The National **Literacy** *Strategy*

Reading and Writing for Information

Activity Resource Bank

Module 6

Oxford University Press

DfEE

Department for
Education and Employment

Contents

Reading and Writing for Information - KS1 and KS2   3

Year R   5

Year 1   10

Year 2   18

Year 3   25

Year 4   32

Year 5   42

Year 6   48

Photocopiable resource sheets
Year R   57
Year 1   59
Year 2   64
Year 3   69
Year 4   74
Year 5   84
Year 6   86

Oxford University Press, Great Clarendon Street, Oxford OX2 6DP

Oxford New York
Athens Auckland Bangkok Bogotá Buenos Aires Calcutta
Cape Town Chennai Dar es Salaam Delhi Florence Hong Kong Istanbul
Karachi Kuala Lumpur Madrid Melbourne Mexico City Mumbai
Nairobi Paris São Paulo Singapore Taipei Tokyo Toronto Warsaw

and associated companies in Berlin Ibadan

Oxford is a registered trade mark of Oxford University Press

© Crown copyright 1998
Produced by Oxford University Press 1998
First published 1998
Reprinted 1999

ISBN 0 19 918957 9

Typeset and designed by Ray Barker, Glen Franklin, Catherine Miller of the
National Literacy Association
Printed in Great Britain

National Literacy Strategy Activity Resource Bank: Reading and Writing for Information - KS1 and KS2

The following resource sheets provide a bank of suggestions for Reading and Writing for Information at Key Stages 1 and 2. They include the sample sheets from the National Literacy Strategy Training Pack, and cover a selection of termly objectives. They are not complete 'Literacy Hours' because they focus on Text level only, although some activities do refer to opportunities for Word and Sentence level work. Some sheets contain a list of resource suggestions as well. They are simply examples of books that teachers have found useful, or that children have enjoyed and which illustrate the objective in an accessible way. **This is in no way prescriptive.** What matters are the outcomes.

All our children need to be able to use information texts effectively to function within society and to learn. This demands:
- the use of a range of reading strategies, e.g. scanning, skimming, close reading;
- an ability to use specific reference and study skills appropriately, e.g. using an index, taking notes;
- an understanding of the function of textual features, e.g. headings, bullet points;
- the ability to interpret a range of graphic information sources, e.g. diagrams, charts, grids;
- an awareness that information in texts is not necessarily accurate and therefore needs to be read critically;
- an ability to write for a range of purposes and audiences using a range of non-fiction texts;
- an understanding of how to read and use more formal registers and technical vocabulary.

The non-fiction activity sheets aim to provide teachers with contextualised, lively and worthwhile ways to support and develop children's growing understanding in these areas.

Progression in the non-fiction strand

Children develop proficiency with literacy through increasingly accurate approximation. For example, their early attempts at writing instructions may contain a mixture of commands ('Put in the soil') and recount ('Then I put in the seed'). Through continued experience of reading and writing instruction texts, along with explicit teaching, childrens' expertise will improve. Thus different non-fiction experiences are revisited throughout the Key Stages. It is also important to realise that it is worth sharing sophisticated non-fiction texts from an early age if these are mediated through teacher-led, shared text work with a class or group. We know that children are able to work at a higher level when supported by a more expert adult than when working independently. Although the children may not independently use new aspects of texts immediately after they have been introduced, they will gradually internalise the concepts and begin to use them without direct teacher mediation.

An overview of the non-fiction teaching programme

In the framework of teaching objectives particular non-fiction types of text are first introduced and then revisited. There is termly focus on a particular type, e.g. recount, but within each term *a wide range of types* will naturally occur within English work and within other curriculum areas. Children will also read and write information texts that contain *a mixture of genres*. For example, a recount of an activity may also contain an explanation as to why the activity was undertaken. We need to be sensitive to the complexities of texts and avoid over-simplification and a rigid set of rules. The guiding principle should be: *What is the purpose of this text and how do we use language to help us achieve that purpose?*

The structures and language features of some important non-fiction text types

The framework overleaf indicates structures and features for text investigation and discussion. It is *not* a rigid set of rules, e.g. a historic recount would be in the past tense.

Our thanks to Widgit Software for permission to use © graphics from their *Writing With Symbols* software package.

Recount

Purpose: to retell events.

Generic structure

- Orientation - 'scene setting' opening, e.g. *I went to the shop …*
- Events - recount of the events as they occurred, e.g. *I saw a vase …*
- Reorientation - a closing statement, e.g. *When I got back I, told my mum.*

Language features of recounts

- Written in the past tense, e.g. *I went.*
- In chronological order, using temporal connectives, e.g. *then, next, after, that.*
- Focus on individual or group participants, e.g. *we, I.*

Procedural

Purpose: to describe how something is done through a series of sequenced steps.

Generic structure

- Goal - a statement of what is to be achieved, e.g. *How to make a sponge cake.*
- Materials/equipment needed, e.g. *2 eggs, flour*
- Sequenced steps to achieve the goal, e.g. *Cream the sugar and butter.*
- Often there is a diagram or illustration.

Language features of procedures

- Written in the present tense or imperative, e.g. *First you sift the flour* or *Sift the flour*
- In chronological order, e.g. first, next
- Focus on generalised human agents rather than named individuals.

Report

Purpose: to describe the way things are.

Generic structure

- An opening, general classification, e.g. *Sparrows are birds.*
- More technical classification (optional), e.g. *Their Latin name is …*
- A description of the phenomenon, including some or all of its:
  qualities, e.g. 'Birds have feathers'
  parts and their function, e.g. 'The beak is …'
  habits/behaviour or uses, e.g. 'They nest in …'

Language features of reports

- Written in the present tense, e.g. *they nest.*
- Non-chronological.
- Focus on generic participants.

Persuasion

Purpose: to argue the case for a point of view.

Generic structure

- Thesis - an opening statement, e.g. *Vegetables are good for you.*
- Arguments - often in the form of point plus elaboration e.g. *They contain vitamins. Vitamin C is vital for …*
- Reiteration - summary and restatement of the opening position, e.g. We have seen that … so …

Language features of persuasion

- The present tense.
- Focus mainly on generic participants.
- Mainly logical rather than temporal connectives, e.g. *this shows, however, because.*

Explanation

Purpose: to explain the processes involved in natural and social phenomena or to explain how something works.

Generic structure

- General statement to introduce the topic, e.g. *In the autumn some birds migrate.*
- A series of logical steps explaining how or why something occurs. e.g. *Because hours of daylight shorten …*
- These steps continue until the final state is produced or the explanation is complete.

Language features of explanation

- Written in the present tense, e.g. *go.*
- Uses temporal connectives, e.g. *then, next,* and/or causal connectives, e.g. *because, so, this causes.*

Discussion

Purpose: to present arguments and information from differing viewpoints.

Generic structure

- Statement of the issue plus a preview of the main arguments.
- Arguments for, plus supporting evidence.
- Arguments against, plus supporting evidence (alternatively, argument/counter argument, one point at a time).
- Recommendation - summary and conclusion.

Language features of discussion

- The present tense.
- Generic human (or non-human) participants.
- Logical connectives, e.g. *therefore, however.*

NLS Activity Resource Sheet

Year	R
Term	
Strand	T 1

Objectives

To recognise printed and hand-written words in a variety of settings, e.g. stories, notes, registers, labels, signs, notices, letters, forms, lists, directions, advertisements, newspapers.

Activities

Class
- Take the class on a Language Walk.
- Point out print in the environment. Talk about the signs, symbols and labels you can see.
- Use a range of early strategies, i.e. initial letters, shapes of words, reading pictures, prediction, context, to encourage recognition.

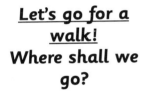

Let's go for a walk!
Where shall we go?

to the park,
around the school,
to the supermarket,
to the headteacher's room,
down the road.

Group
- Make cards for the children to play matching games with signs, symbols and labels, relating to the types of labels they have seen on their walk.
- Ask the children to make signs and labels for the classroom in a similar style to those they saw on their walk, e.g. entry signs, warnings, instructions for use.

Relevant published materials/resources

NLS Activity Resource Sheet

Year	R
Term	
Strand	T 1

Objectives

To recognise printed and handwritten words in a variety of settings, e.g. stories, notes, registers, labels, signs, notices, letters, forms, lists, directions, adverts, newspapers.

Activities

N.B.
It is important to draw children's attention to many types of environmental print, emphasising the purpose and audience.
This can be provided through structured role-play.

Class

● Explain that you are setting up a new role-play area, e.g. a cafe, and provide every opportunity to involve the children in its planning and development. Talk about what you might find in a cafe.

● If possible, plan a visit to a cafe. Draw attention to examples of print.

● In a Shared Writing session decide collaboratively on appropriate signs and labels.

Waiter, the bill please!

Group

● During their time in the role-play area give the children clear tasks to encourage the purposeful use of print, e.g.
Change the menu in the cafe.
Order a meal.
Write a cheque to pay the bill.
Advertise a new dessert on the menu.

Some suggestions for role-play areas

Specific shops - shoe shop, grocer's, supermarket.
Services - doctor's surgery, baby clinic, garage, hairdresser, cafe, library, travel agency, museum, factory, airport, railway station, post office, laundry, school.

Relevant published materials/resources

NLS Activity Resource Sheet

Year	R
Term	
Strand	T 1

To understand and use correctly terms about books and print: *book, cover, beginning, end, page, line, word, letter, title.*

Activities

N.B.
This is also a good opportunity to introduce the terminology *non-fiction* for information and *fiction* for a story.

Class

● Using a shared Big Book, feign ignorance, e.g. hold the book upside down; start with the back facing; pretend not to know where to start reading. Encourage the children to correct your mistakes.

● Ask direct questions, e.g. *Who can show me where to start reading?, Which way do I go?*

● Encourage prediction from the title and cover. Ask, *What do you think the book will be about?*

● Use the correct terminology from the beginning and provide opportunities to use the correct terminology in context.

Group

● Make a simple information book, e.g. folded A4 paper. Ask the children to think of a title, e.g. *My Family*, and to design the front cover. These could then be written in shared or individual writing sessions.

● Ask the children to classify books, e.g. after a farm visit find four books with animals on the cover. Ask, *Which are fiction? Which are non-fiction? How can you tell?*

Relevant published materials/resources

NLS Activity Resource Sheet

Year	R
Term	
Strand	T 11

Objectives

To distinguish between writing and drawing in books and in own work.

Activities

N.B.
Young children may not understand the conventions of labelling diagrams and may confuse the meaning of the line which links words to the diagram. They may see this line as part of the diagram or word.
The use of a different material, e.g. thread, or colour, can help make the function of this line clearer to them.

Class

● Using Big Books during Shared Reading, ask direct questions, e.g. *Can you show me a word? Where are the words? Where is the picture? What kind of picture is this?* i.e. photograph, drawing, diagrams.
● Discuss what the children can tell from the pictures. Point out examples where the words confirm what is in the pictures.
● Provide a range of different visual sources available in the classroom, e.g. pictures, charts.
● In Shared Writing, the children can decide on labels for the pictures around the room.

Group

● Provide sheets with clearly defined areas for writing and picture or use Photocopiable Resource Sheet A.
● Provide some diagrams, e.g. body parts, the face, or use Photocopiable Resource Sheet B. The children write the labels.
● The children write labels for their own drawings.
● Make picture-only accounts of events.
● Add words to wordless non-fiction books, e.g. some board books can have captions or labels added, *This is a house.*

Relevant published materials/resources

Big wordless books, e.g. **Collins Primary English Big Book** (Collins Ed.), **Nine to Five Infoactive** (Collins). Use Big Books which have photographs, drawings and diagrams, e.g.**The Book Project** (Longman), **All Aboard** (Ginn), **Oxford Reading Tree** (OUP) and non-fiction Big Books, e.g. **Infoactive** (Collins Educational), **Reading Science** (Nelson), **Discovery World** (Heinemann).

NLS Activity Resource Sheet

Year	R
Term	
Strand	T 12

Objectives

To experiment with writing in a variety of play, exploratory and role-play situations.

Activities

N.B.
This activity relates to a class visit, e.g. to a farm (links with **YR W11**).
All writing activities are preceded by extensive work with whole class. Most of this will be oral work often with the teacher as scribe.
The group task should be structured to allow children to communicate ideas to lots of audiences. Group and individual writing must be aided by *Breakthrough*, word banks or similar support materials.

Class

● Encourage the children to retell the story of the visit. Model the sequence of the story, e.g. *What did we do first?* pulling out key words.
● Ask, *What did you think you were going to see?*, *What did you see?*, *Were you surprised?*.
● In Shared Reading look at stories and non-fiction texts related to a farm visit.

I'm a horse and I eat grass!

Group

● Ask the children to draw or paint a picture of the most important event which happened during the visit.
● Give the children a selection of photographs to sequence and add their own captions. These can then be made into a group book.
● The children use photographs or their own paintings of animals and add speech bubbles.
● Using soft toys, each child takes on the role of an animal, and tells the group facts about itself.

Plenary

● The children share their paintings and drawings of the most important event.
● The class decide on captions and sequencing. The teacher scribes captions for the pictures.

Relevant published materials/resources

The Farm Concert, Story Chest series (Kingscourt). **The Life of a Duck,** Magic Bean In-Fact (Heinemann). **Who's in the Shed?** Literacy Links (Kingscourt). **Farmer Duck,** Martin Wadell (Walker Books). A collection of soft toy farm animals.

NLS Activity Resource Sheet

Year	1
Term	1
Strand	T 12,14

To read and use captions, e.g. labels around the school, on equipment.
To write captions for their own work, e.g. for display, in class books.

Activities

Class

● Build up a class display of objects on various themes, e.g. pets.
● Ask the children to identify the objects and say something about them.
● In Shared Writing use the children's comments and write the captions. Ask the children to attach them to the display.
● The display can be used at later sessions for reinforcement (link with **Y1 T1 W8**).

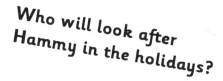

Who will look after Hammy in the holidays?

My hamster eats seeds.

Don't forget to change the water.

We know all about hamsters

Group

● Read around the room using captions.
● Write captions related to a display activity in shared sessions (link with **Y1 T1 S4**).
● The group could produce a book related to the display, so that at the end of a term each group will have made a reference book on a particular theme.

Plenary

● The children share the captions they have been writing.

Relevant published materials/resources

Infoactive (Collins Ed.). **Reading Science** series (Nelson). **Day and Night Animals** and **My Body**, Discovery World (Heinemann).

NLS Activity Resource Sheet

Year	1
Term	1
Strand	T 14 – 16

Objectives

To write captions for their own work, e.g. for display, in class books. To make simple lists for planning, reminding, etc. To write and draw simple instructions and labels for everday classroom use, e.g. in role-play area, for equipment.

N.B.
See also **Y1 T1 S4**: To write captions and simple sentences, and to re-read, recognising whether or not they make sense.

Activities

Class

- Model writing captions and instructions through Shared Writing and computer text, e.g. *Task for today. Labels for tables. Make a book. Do some handwriting. Our classroom rules.*
- Model use of weather charts, etc.
- Change written instructions into organisational devices, using graphics, e.g. *Feed the fish* instructions become:

Group

- Investigate and collect examples of captions in the school environment.
- Generate instructions for class use, e.g.
How to ... feed fish/other pets, use a computer, the book area, etc.
Don't forget ... book changing day, day for swimming kit/PE kit, turn off the lights, etc.
- Use the Plenary session for re-reading sentences and captions.
- Produce final drafts in a Guided Writing session, focusing on children's best writing. Act as scribe or use a talking word processor to generate text.

- Generate own picture instructions for class display.
- Provide a resource sheet to indicate relationships. See the Photocopiable Resource Sheet.

On	We
Mon	TV ☐
Tue	PE
Wed	Swim
Thurs	Sing
Fri	

Relevant published materials/resources

Infoactive (Collins Ed.). **Discovery World** (Heinemann).

NLS Activity Resource Sheet

Objectives

To read and follow simple instructions, e.g. for classroom routines, lists for groups in workbooks; to write and draw simple instructions and labels for everyday classroom use, e.g. in role-play area, for equipment.

Activities

Class

● Pick a subject, e.g. class rules, and in Shared Writing brainstorm and scribe the children's suggestions.

● Focus on the different forms, e.g. *You must not run, We walk sensibly in class, Only three people in the book corner.*

● Plan posters or captions.

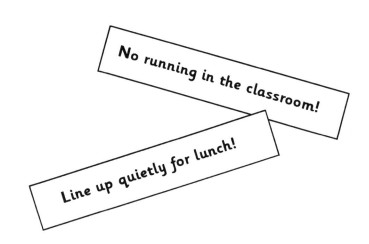

No running in the classroom!

Line up quietly for lunch!

You could write instructions for:

putting out the P.E. apparatus;
changing reading books;
taking care of the art equipment;
using the computer;
feeding/cleaning pets.

Group

● The groups make a *rules* poster (link with **Y1 T1 Sentence work**).

Plenary

● Check the effectiveness of the rules. Ask, *Do the instructions work? Do we need to change anything? Which posters are more effective?*

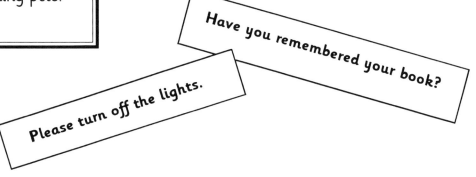

Have you remembered your book?

Please turn off the lights.

Relevant published materials/resources

NLS Activity Resource Sheet

Year	1
Term	2
Strand	T 17

Objectives

To use terms 'fiction' and 'non-fiction', noting some of their differing features, e.g. layout, titles, contents page, use of pictures, labelled diagrams.

Activities

Class

● Using Big Book examples of fiction and non-fiction, draw the children's attention to cover details, i.e. photos, illustrations, title, author.

● Look at the features of a non-fiction book together and compile a list. Look for similar features in a fiction text. What is the same? What is different?

Looking at non-fiction

title
author
index
contents
glossary
photographs
diagrams

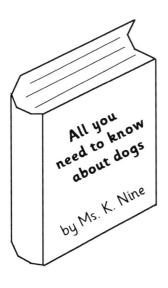

All you need to know about dogs

by Ms. K. Nine

Group

● Ask the children to sort a variety of books into two collections: fiction and non-fiction.

● The groups select books from the book corner or the library, according to a given topic, e.g. farm animals.

● Explore classification of books, e.g. a selection of non-fiction books, into subjects/topics, according to features.

Plenary

● Encourage the children to explain their criteria for selection.

● Start to produce a wall chart entitled, *What we know about non-fiction.*

Relevant published materials/resources

Any non fiction Big Books, e.g. **Oxford Reading Tree** series (OUP), **Reading Science** (Nelson), **Infoactive** (Collins), **All Aboard** (Ginn), **Book Project** (Longman), **Magic Bean In-Fact** (Heinemann), **Discovery World** (Heinemann).

NLS Activity Resource Sheet

Year	1
Term	2
Strand	T 18,19,21

Objectives

To read non-fiction books and understand that the reader ... selects according to what is needed; to predict what a given book might be about from a brief look at both front and back covers ... ; to understand the purpose of content pages and indexes and to begin to locate information by page numbers and words by initial letter.

Activities

N.B.
Skills first taught within the Literacy Hour can then be consolidated and extended through class topics and other curricular areas.

Class

● Mask the front cover photo and title of a non-fiction Big Book with strips of paper. Reveal the photo by removing paper strips one by one, encouraging the children to predict the subject matter of the photo.

● Ask the children to predict the title, revealing the individual words either for clues or to confirm predictions. Discuss and list possible content suggestions.

● Ask the children to suggest questions that they think will be answered in the book. List these on a flip chart. Use the contents page to identify sections where the information will be found.

● Ask the children to suggest words that they think will be found in the book. Use the index to look up the words and model how to locate the information by initial letters and page numbers.

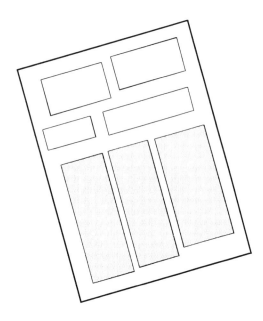

Group

● The children can carry out the activities above as part of Guided Reading with an unfamiliar text or as an independent activity.

Plenary

● Refer back to content predictions.

Relevant published materials/resources

Any non-fiction Big Books, e.g. **Oxford Reading Tree** series (OUP), **Reading Science** (Nelson), **Infoactive** (Collins), **All Aboard** (Ginn), **The Book Project** (Longman), **Magic Bean** (Heinemann).

NLS Activity Resource Sheet

Objectives

To use simple dictionaries, and to understand their alphabetical organisation.

Activities

Class

● Enlarge an extract from a simple dictionary to A3 or on OHT and model the use of a dictionary.

● Explore features of layout and use initial letter sounds to locate words.

● Demonstrate how to look up a word during Shared Reading or Writing.

Group

● Give the children a variety of pictures and words. Ask them to find these words in a dictionary.

● Begin a class dictionary, possibly linked to a class topic.

Relevant published materials/resources

Collins Picture Dictionary (Harper Collins). **ABC Big Book, Pathways** (Collins). **My First Oxford Dictionary** (OUP). Alphabet friezes.

NLS Activity Resource Sheet

Year	1
Term	2
Strand	T 25,W10

Objectives

To assemble information from own experience; to use simple sentences to describe, based on examples from reading; to write simple, non-chronological reports and to organise in lists, separate pages, charts. To make collections of ... significant words linked to particular topics.

Activities

Class

- Using artefacts, books, etc. as a stimulus, ask the children to contribute what they know about the item. Use questions to focus on specific details.
- In a modelled writing session, using the questions as headings, demonstrate how to construct simple sentences using the children's information e.g. *Apples can be eaten.*

QUESTIONS TO SUPPORT NON-CHRONOLOGICAL REPORT WRITING

What is it?
What does it look like?
Where is it found?
What is it used for?

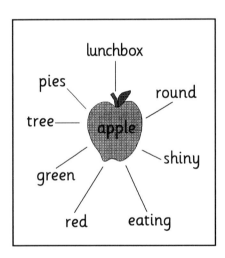

Group

- Using an artefact or pictures drawn on an A3 sheet, follow the above points as a group.
- Provide writing frameworks for the children to complete, ranging from headings to more structured cloze texts, e.g. *An --- is a fruit.* Use the Photocopiable Resource Sheet if required.
- Using the collections of words, build word banks linked to topics. Put individual words on cards.
- Encourage the children to read and re-read them, match and sort.

Plenary

- When all the groups have completed the activities, discuss how the writing might be collated into a class reference book, e.g. alphabetically.

Relevant published materials/resources

NLS Activity Resource Sheet

Objectives

To recognise that non-fiction books on similar themes can give different information and present similar information in different ways. To identify simple questions and use text to find answers. To locate parts of text that give particular information including labelled diagrams and charts. To write own questions prior to reading for information and to record answers.

Activities

N.B.
This is a holistic approach which integrates all these strands. It will take about two weeks. The same activity is then revisited later in the term (using a different theme/topic) to reinforce the concepts/skills.
Week one will be teacher-led, whole-class activities only. The group activities come in week two of the cycle.

See the Photocopiable Resource Sheets for an exemplar lesson plan and recording pro formas.

Relevant published materials/resources

You will need two information books and one story book on the same topic, e.g. **The Life of a Duck,** Magic Bean In-Fact (Heinemann), **Duck Diary,** Literacy Links (Kingscourt), **Farmer Duck,** Martin Wadell (Walker Books).

NLS Activity Resource Sheet

Year	2
Term	1
Strand	T 13,14

Objectives

To read simple written instructions in the classroom, simple recipes, plans, instructions for constructing something. To note key structural features, e.g. clear statement of purpose at start, sequential steps set out in a list, direct language.

Activities

N.B.
You will need to collect a wide range of examples of instructions/direction type texts including some exceptions, e.g. those which are purely diagrammatical.

Class

Using an instructional Big Book, e.g. a recipe book:
● Pull out key features of an instruction text, e.g. sequence stages, instructional language, listing resources, numbering, bullet points, different ways of presenting information.
● Cut up an example of an instruction text and re-order it with the class.
● Look at examples of recipes, tins, signs, packets.

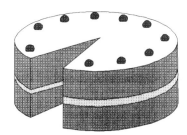

Group

● Use the key features grid on the Photocopiable Resource Sheet to explore instructional texts.
● Re-order the cut up examples.
● Practise reading instructional texts, identifying and listing the key words, e.g. useful words for writing a recipe.

Plenary

● Look for exceptions to the key features.
● Make a class list of key words for recipes, instructions for making something, etc. Use these as a basis for display.

Relevant published materials/resources

Making Puppets, Magic Bean In-Fact (Heinemann). **The Make a Book Book,** Pathways (Collins Ed.).

NLS Activity Resource Sheet

Year	
Term	
Strand	

Objectives

To write simple instructions, e.g. getting to school, playing a game.

Activities

Class
- Model instructions with a text, e.g. **On The Way Home,** or any other text using directional language, e.g. *under, past, beside*, and prepositions.
- As a Shared Writing task, write the instructions for moving from one part of the school to another. Focus on the sequence, particular language and prepositions.
- Walk the route with the children and emphasise the key points and language, e.g. through the hall, past the library.
- Review the walk back in class and list the key words

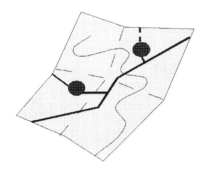

Relevant published materials/resources

NLS Activity Resource Sheet

Year	2
Term	1
Strand	T 15,16

Objectives

To write simple instructions, e.g. getting to school, playing a game.
To use models from reading to organise instructions sequentially, e.g. listing points in order, each point depending on the previous one, numbering.

Activities

N.B.
Children need extensive prior experience of reading and following rules for games in group activities in class.

Class

- Revise the key features of instruction texts, e.g. sequence, instructional language, list of resources.
- Look at examples from books and games.
- Play a simple known game with the class. Identify the key features, e.g. aim, resources, players, rules, what happens if you cheat, what counts as cheating.
- Brainstorm the rules for the game. Put into a simple sequence or order. Give the key words.

Group

- Play a familiar game.
- Discuss and agree on the sequence of activities.
- Write each action on a piece of card.
- Order these in the correct sequence, adjusting and adding to as necessary.
- Transfer these to a writing frame, or use the Photocopiable Resource Sheet in a Shared Writing session, supported by an adult.
- Give the rules to another group to evaluate.

Plenary

- Each group feeds back about how successful the instructions were and makes alterations where necessary.

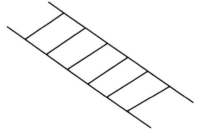

Relevant published materials/resources

Making Puppets, Magic Bean In-Fact (Heinemann). **Writing Frames,** Maureen Lewis and David Wray (Reading and Language Information Centre, Reading University). **The Make a Book Book,** Pathways (Collins Ed.).

NLS Activity Resource Sheet

Objectives

To use diagrams in instructions, e.g. drawing and labelling diagrams as part of a set of instructions.

Activities

Class

● Using a Big Book in a Shared Reading session, explore the differences between photographs, diagrams and drawings, clarifying the specific features.

● Look at how items are labelled, e.g. straight lines between the label and the diagram, labels as single words.

● Label a class display, emphasising different aspects.

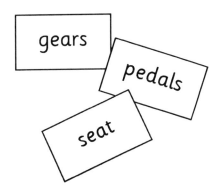

gears

pedals

seat

Group

● Give the children a selection of pictures and diagrams to label. You may want to give the group a few key words to start with.

● The children think of other words and write their own labels.

Plenary

● Discuss whether it is easier to label a photograph or diagram.

● One group of children could share their labelled pictures. The rest of the class list alternative, additional words that could be used.

wheels

spokes

Relevant published materials/resources

Which is Which?, Magic Bean in Fact (Heinemann). **Life of a Duck,** Magic Bean In-Fact (Heinemann). **Check up with the Doctor,** Magic Bean In-Fact (Heinemann). **Infoactive** (Collins Educational). **Discovery Worlds** (Heinemann).

NLS Activity Resource Sheet

Objectives

To understand that dictionaries and glossaries give definitions and explanations; discuss what definitions are, explore some simple definitions in dictionaries. To use other alphabetically ordered texts, e.g. indexes, directories, listings, registers; to discuss how they are used.

Activities

Class

- Enlarge a page from a dictionary or use an OHT of a dictionary page.
- Model how to use the dictionary.
- Discuss what dictionaries are used for, e.g. to check spellings, to give definitions.
- Explore how they are organised, e.g. at whole book level, individual entry level, word pronunciation, definition.
- Demonstrate how to use dictionaries.

Aa   apple

Group

- Generate a list of words linked to a topic.
- Arrange alphabetically.
- Each member of the group takes a word, illustrates it, writes a definition and then checks it in a dictionary.
- Use the Photocopiable Resource Sheet as a writing frame if required.

Plenary

- Assemble the definitions alphabetically as a class dictionary frieze around the room. Insert blanks if no word has been found for a particular letter.
- Discuss the beginning, middle and end sections of the alphabet and ask which sections different letters can be found in.
- Play a dictionary game. Call out a word and a child's name. The child runs to the word and reads the definition.

N.B.
This activity helps to begin to form an understanding of the beginning, middle and end of the alphabet and supports the children when using book-form dictionaries.
They can turn to the end or the middle, etc., rather than always starting from the beginning.

Relevant published materials/resources

ABC Big Book, Collins Pathways (Collins Educational). A range of dictionaries, from simple picture dictionaries to more complex examples. Alphabet friezes.

NLS Activity Resource Sheet

Year	2
Term	3
Strand	T 13

Objectives

To understand the distinction between fact and fiction; to use terms 'fact', 'fiction' and 'non-fiction' appropriately.

Activities

Class

● Using a non-fiction Big Book, explore the typical features and produce a class list of questions that would identify a text as non-fiction.

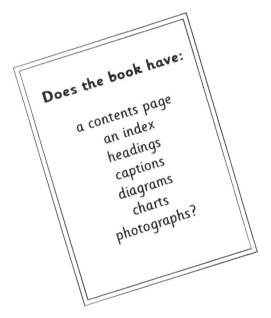

Does the book have:

a contents page
an index
headings
captions
diagrams
charts
photographs?

Group

● The children select a number of non-fiction books from the book corner. Using the Photocopiable Resource Sheet or their own questions, they can check whether their books have the listed features.
● Encourage the children to feed back as to the effectiveness of the books, i.e. do they have supportive features such as an index, contents, etc.
● Using photocopied extracts from books, newspapers, magazines, etc., ask the children to identify those that are non-fiction, marking the statements, terms and words that lead them to this decision.

Relevant published materials/resources

NLS Activity Resource Sheet

Year	2
Term	3
Strand	T 14 – 17

Objectives

To pose questions ... prior to reading non-fiction to find answers. To use a contents page and index to find way around text. To scan a text to find specific questions. To skim-read title, contents page, illustrations, chapter headings and sub-headings to speculate what a book might be about.

Activities

N.B.
See also **Y2 T3 T19**: To make simple notes from non-fiction texts, e.g. key words and phrases, page references, headings, to use in subsequent writing.

Class

● Using a non-fiction Big Book, explore the title and the front cover, possibly masking the title and asking the children to predict from the cover. Discuss what they might expect to find in the text.
● Refer to the contents page. Explain how this is used.
● Ask the class to brainstorm five words related to the topic. Check these words in the index and model how it is used.
● Explore the layout of the book and select one section. Brainstorm with the children four questions you might ask about the information in the section.
● Make explicit the key words in the questions and locate key words in the text.
● Read the section and model answering the questions in order to identify the main points in the passage.
● From an enlarged section of text, frame questions and highlight the key words and phrases in those questions.
● Ask the children to identify whether the same key words and phrases are in the text.

birds
branches
roots
leaves
seasons

Do the leaves of an oak tree fall in winter?

Group

● Give each child a simple photocopied extract of non-fiction text with a clear heading.
● Ask the children to devise five or six questions that might be answered in the text.
● The children read the text, refining their questions and rephrasing those that were not answered in the text.
● The children highlight key words and phrases in their questions and in the text.
● On a large sheet they write out the answers to their questions.

Relevant published materials/resources

NLS Activity Resource Sheet

Year	3
Term	1
Strand	T 16,17

Objectives

To understand the disctinction between fact and fiction; to use the terms 'fact', 'fiction' and 'non-fiction' appropriately. To notice differences in the style and structure of fiction and non-fiction writing.

N.B.
You will need to select two books with which the children are familiar, one fiction, one non-fiction.
There may be a link with other curriculum areas, e.g. historical era, setting, scientific process.

Activities

Class
● Model comparison of the books you have selected, developing a matrix for use in group work, e.g. predict content, purpose for reading. Ask, *Why might someone read this book?*
● Explore the features of the books, e.g. chapters, contents page, index.
● Are there any drawings, diagrams or photographs? Any dialogue or characters?
● Look at headings, sub-headings with text, different sizes of print, use of bold italics, capitalisation, etc.

Group
● Sort sets of books and complete Photocopiable Resource Sheet A.
● Predict the content by examining the cover. Check by opening the book in the middle. Use Photocopiable Resource Sheet B.
● Design book covers, blurbs and chapter headings for parallel fiction and non-fiction books, e.g. about Victorians, or computers.
● Compare three non-fiction and three fiction texts on the same topic, e.g. **Goldilocks and the Three Bears, We're Going on a Bear Hunt, Can't You Sleep, Little Bear?**, and three non-fiction books about bears. Complete Photocopiable Resource Sheet C.

Plenary
● Explore the fact that simply saying that fiction is not true and non-fiction is true is too simple. Look at the facts that are learnt from some fiction stories. Find contradictions in non-fiction books.

Relevant published materials/resources

Goldilocks, Traditional. **We're Going on a Bear Hunt,** Michael Rosen (Walker). **Can't You Sleep Little Bear?,** Martin Waddell (Walker).

NLS Activity Resource Sheet

Year	3
Term	1
Strand	T 18

Objectives

To locate information, using contents, index, headings, sub-headings, page nos., bibliographies.

Activities

Class
- Select a relevant Big Book with key features of information texts.
Explore contents, index, headings, pictures, diagrams.
- Model for the children how reading information texts differs from reading
a story, i.e. locating what you want to read rather than reading from beginning
to end.
- Ask:
  - *What do I want to find out about?*
  - *Which of these books would contain relevant information?*
  - *How do I look? Where do I look first?*
- Talk about how pictures and diagrams provide information as well as the text.
Look at illustrations and diagrams in text.
- Demonstrate how, having found the page through using the contents and index
pages, you use headings, scanning and locating key words.

Group
- With a question to answer, the children practise identifying, locating and reading
aloud from books independently.

Plenary
- The children take on the role of teacher with the class group, showing how they
found their information.

Relevant published materials/resources

Magic Bean In-Fact series (Heinemann). **Literacy Links Plus** (Kingscourt). **Discovery World** (Heinemann).

NLS Activity Resource Sheet

Objectives

To write simple, non-chronological reports from known information, e.g. from own experience or from texts read, using notes made to organise and present ideas. Write for a known audience, e.g. other pupils in the class, teacher, parent.

Activities

Class

● In a Modelled Writing session, begin with brainstorming and planning. Ask, *What do we know about ...,* e.g.

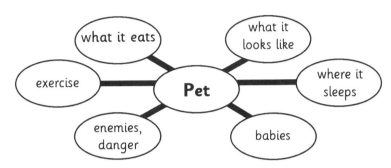

● Model moving from this to writing a descriptive report. Provide a writing frame, as on the Photocopiable Resource Sheet, if necessary.

Group

● Ask the children to select an animal or pet they know about. Brainstorm and list all the facts they know in a web or puddle diagram. Use the headings to organise their facts and create a draft.
● Share the drafts and discuss, e.g. *Have we used headings? How have we organised the information?*
● Revise, proof read and publish the work as a class book. Use writing frames with groups who may need support to introduce each section.
● To move on to individual report writing, ask the children to select a topic they know about. They brainstorm and list what they know. They create headings in pairs, e.g. *Title or introduction, what it is, what it does, what it uses* and *a concluding statement.* These need to be checked by the teacher. The children then make notes under their headings and use their notes to write a draft. Discuss with response partners. Proof read and publish in individual booklets, e.g. Zig Zag booklets.

Relevant published materials/resources

First Steps Writing Resource Book (Heinemann), Chapter six provides very useful reading and writing activities related to report writing. **Writing Frames** Maureen Lewis and David Wray (Reading and Language Information Centre, Reading University).

NLS Activity Resource Sheet

Year	3
Term	2
Strand	T 12

Objectives

To identify the different purposes of instructional texts, e.g. recipes, route-finders, timetables, instructions, plans, rules.

Activities

N.B.
You will need a collection of a wide range of authentic texts, e.g. food packets, recipe cards, appointment reminders, rules of board games, TV listings, train timetables, supermarket leaflets, junk mail.

Class

● Play *Text Lucky Dip*. Mix all the texts in a bag. Each child takes one at random and is invited to say what it is, what they think its purpose is and who it is written for. The teacher scribes the responses on a chart. See the Photocopiable Resource Sheet.

Text	Purpose (why written)	Audience (who for)

● Ask if any of the other children hold a text with a similar purpose. Add these to the chart. Then move on to a new text from another child. Display the charts and texts around the classroom.

Group

● In pairs, the children go through a newspaper or magazine and find a given number of different texts, each of which has a different purpose, e.g. weather forecast, cartoon strip. Cut out the texts, or an extract and stick onto the first column of the chart.

Relevant published materials/resources

NLS Activity Resource Sheet

Year	3
Term	2
Strand	T 14

Objectives

How written instructions are organised, e.g. lists, numbered points, diagrams with arrows, bullet points, keys.

Activities

Class

● Have enlarged versions of instruction texts and annotate if possible. Examine examples of instructions and draw the children's attention to the structure of the text, i.e.

 - the aim or goal, explicit or implied, e.g. Chocolate Cake implies that this will be the instructions for making a chocolate cake;
 - equipment and materials required;
 - what to do, usually in chronological order, possibly with diagrams or pictures for clarification.

● Discuss the structure and why it is important, e.g. why does it need to be in the correct order?

● Examine ways in which the correct order is signalled, e.g. numbering/lettering; use of time words, such as next, then, after.

● Explore the use of graphics to signal time order, e.g. arrows, lists, bullet points.

Group

● Give pairs of children cut up or jumbled instructions. Ask them to reassemble these in the correct order.

● Give instructions in one format, e.g. a recipe as a visual flow chart. The children reformat this, e.g. as written, numbered instructions.

Relevant published materials/resources

Making Puppets and **Keeping Silkworms,** Magic Bean In-Fact series (Heinemann).
The Make a Book Book, Collins Pathways (Collins Ed.).

NLS Activity Resource Sheet

Year	3
Term	2
Strand	T 16

Objectives

To write instructions, e.g. rules for playing games, recipes, using a range of organisational devices, e.g. lists, dashes, commas for lists in sentences, recognising the importance of correct sequence; use 'writing frames' as appropriate for support. Links with **Y3 T2 T14.**

Activities

Class
- Model the writing of a set of instructions, explaining the language and structure chosen.
- In a Shared Writing session, encourage the children to offer suggestions for the structure and language of an instructional text.
- As a whole class, edit the piece of Shared Writing.

Group
- Ask the children to write instructional texts, following the framework discussed previously.
- Encourage them to discuss the sequence of their instructions and their choice of language.

Plenary
- The groups read their instructions to the rest of the class.
- Ask the listeners to see whether they could follow the instructions to achieve the goal.

Relevant published materials/resources

NLS Activity Resource Sheet

Objectives

To read examples of letters written for different purposes ...; understand form and layout ...; to write letters, notes and messages linked to work in other subjects; to communicate within school; letters to authors about books, selecting style and vocabulary appropriate to the intended reader.

Activities

N.B.
Collect examples of letters from children's magazines, newspapers, personal examples, etc.
Make a large postbox-shaped display board.
Do not fix the examples permanently. The display will need to be interactive.

Class

- Use the letter collection to extract the key features, e.g. beginnings, formal or informal ways of addressing recipients.
- Make displays of each of these features, e.g. a collection of letter beginnings or endings.
- Add other examples, e.g. postcards, telemessages, e-mails and faxed messages.

Group

- Using examples of real letters, ask the children to chart the most common beginnings and endings in different types of letters, e.g.

letters to	friends	newspapers	businesses
beginnings			
endings			

- Write letters describing the same event, e.g. a trip to a farm, to:
    - a friend
    - a parent
    - the company that provided the funding to undertake the trip.

Plenary

- Look at the different versions and compare beginnings and endings, font, formal and informal language.
- Discuss the effect of the variations.

Relevant published materials/resources

Dear Sam, Dear Ben, Magic Bean (Heinemann).

NLS Activity Resource Sheet

Objectives

To identify different types of text, e.g. their content, structure, vocabulary, style, lay-out and purpose; to select and examine opening sentences that set scenes, capture interest, etc.; pick out key sentences/phrases that convey information.

Activities

N.B.
You will need to have collected a series of newspaper reports, magazine articles on a topic, e.g. a favourite singer or football team, biographical articles, reviews, reports, gossip.
Start a display and encourage the children to read, comment and add to it.

Class

● Select three different texts from the display. Enlarge copies on OHT or provide multiple copies. Read and discuss each text with the class.
● Use an enlarged copy of the Photocopiable Resource Sheet to identify the purpose, audience, form and important points. Model how to fill in the chart.

Type of text	Purpose	Audience	Most important points
News report from the 'Sun'.	To give information. To entertain or interest the reader.	Grown-ups. Fans.	New album out. Party to celebrate. Lots of famous people there.
Record review in 'Top Hits' magazine.	To give opinion.	Record buyers. Fans.	Six good tracks. Some remix of old material. Thinks will sell well.

Group

● The children use the sheet to look at other items from the display.

Plenary

● Compare the children's charts on the same article. Do they agree or disagree on the purpose, key points?

Relevant published materials/resources

NLS Activity Resource Sheet

Year	4
Term	1
Strand	T 19

Objectives

To understand and use the terms *fact* and *opinion*; and to begin to distinguish the two in reading and other media.

Activities

Class

- Read a selected article from a newspaper with the class, using an enlarged version on OHT or multiple copies.
- Discuss which statements are verifiable facts and underline these in blue.
- Discuss which statements are opinions, feelings, or responses, and underline these in red.
- Draw attention to cues for opinions, e.g. *I think that*, judgement words, e.g. *good, bad, shocking*. Look for words that suggest tentativeness or lack of certainty, e.g. *might, probably*, and for debatable facts.
- Use the Photocopiable Resource Sheet A to model filling in a chart, recording the categories of sentences underlined.
- Discuss what to do about any sentences not underlined.

Group

- Provide a set of pictures from current topic books, newspapers, etc. Ask the children to respond by writing three opinions and three facts. Provide a writing prompt such as: 'From this picture I know that ..., From this picture I think that ...'.
This activity works well with history and geography pictures.
- Alternatively, the children could write facts on one colour, sticky removable notes and opinions on another colour, and surround the picture with these. The notes can then be written up as a prose piece.
- Give the children an account of the same event from different newspapers. Ask them to underline the key facts. Draw up a fact chart. See the Photocopiable Resource Sheet B. Do the facts agree?

Plenary

- Compare the facts and opinions produced by different children using the same picture, and the key facts from different newspapers reporting the same event.

Relevant published materials/resources

NLS Activity Resource Sheet

Year	4
Term	1
Strand	T 21

Objectives

Predict newspaper stories from the evidence of headlines, making notes and then checking against the original.

N.B.
You will need to have collected a variety of newspaper headlines, e.g. some clear, some ambiguous, some jokey, different sizes, different fonts. Use these to make a montage.

Activities

Class

● Using the collection, ask the children to select one. Read it aloud. What do they think it means? Discuss what type of story it is. Explore the choice of words.

Group

● Prepare two sets, one of headlines and the other of articles. Ask the children to match the headlines to the right articles.

● Give the group a selection of articles with the headlines removed. The children add as many different headlines as they can think of. Then they compare their ideas with the original.

● Give the group a selection of headlines only and ask them to write the report to go with it.

● Compare the children's articles with the original.

Relevant published materials/resources

Rescues, Magic Bean In-Fact (Heinemann).

NLS Activity Resource Sheet

Year	4
Term	1
Strand	T 24

Objectives

To write newspaper-style reports, including editing stories to fit a particular space.

Activities

Class
- Select an article and enlarge it on OHT or provide multiple copies.
- Model deleting to shorten the text and continue until only a skeleton outline remains. Discuss the deletions made, e.g. *Why was that section deleted? What was repeated?* Discuss when brevity is important, e.g. *notes, telegrams, faxes, headlines, prompt cards for speech*, and have examples where possible.

Group
- Explain to the children that authors often have to write to a set word limit. Give out some articles and ask the children to shorten them to a given number of words.
- Using the same article, say that it must be shortened again to note form, i.e. as brief as possible.
- Take examples of the children's own writing and ask them to edit down to a set word limit.

Plenary
- Discuss reasons for their editing decisions.

Relevant published materials/resources

NLS Activity Resource Sheet

Objectives

To appraise a non-fiction book for its content and usefulness by scanning, e.g. headings, contents lists. To prepare for factual research by reviewing what is known, what is needed, what is available and where one might search. To scan texts in print or on screen to locate key words or phrases, useful headings and key sentences and to use these as a text for summarising text.

Activities

Class
- Using two or three books on a current topic in science, history or geography, model questioning to encourage prediction using just titles, headings, etc. Scribe the responses.
- Brainstorm what the children know already, e.g. the Romans wore armour.
- Brainstorm questions to research, using Photocopiable Resource Sheet A.

Group
- Collect a variety of assorted books on the theme, e.g. Romans.
- Give one question to each pair of children. Ask them to highlight the key search words in the question, e.g. What kind of *weapons* did the Romans carry?
- Ask the children to select three books from the collection. Use Photocopiable Resource Sheet A to phrase a question. Then use Photocopiable Resource Sheets B and C to assess each book's usefulness in answering the question.

Plenary
- The children recommend a 'best buy' book and explain why. Compare the assessments.
- Explore why a book might be more useful for one question than for another.

Relevant published materials/resources

NLS Activity Resource Sheet

Objectives

To prepare for factual research by reviewing what is known, what is needed, what is available and where one might search. To scan texts in print or on screen to locate key words or phrases, useful headings and key sentences and to use these as a tool for summarising text. Links with **Y4 T2 T15**.

Activities

Class
- Remind the class of question setting and book selection work from **Y4 T2 T15.**
- Using a Big Book with an acetate sheet or an OHT of a non-fiction passage, model how to scan the text for key words, underlining key points.
- Demonstrate note-taking on a flip chart.

Group
- Working in pairs, with a question to answer, the children chose two of their 'best buy' books from activity **Y4 T2 T15** to answer their question. If resources allow, encourage the children to select a relevant page, photocopy it and text mark. Use Photocopiable Resource Sheets A, B or C to record notes.

Plenary
- Compare the children's notes with the book texts. Discuss how these vary. Discuss what has been deleted, omitted and why.
- Explore what it is that makes good note-taking effective.

Relevant published materials/resources

NLS Activity Resource Sheet

Year	4
Term	2
Strand	T 21 – 23

Objectives

To make short notes, e.g. by abbreviating ideas, selecting key words, listing or in diagrammatic form. To fill out brief notes into connected prose. To collect information from a variety of sources and present it in one simple format, e.g. wall chart, labelled diagram.

Activities

Class

● Using an enlarged version of a completed note-taking grid from **Y4 T2 T16, 17**, model a Shared Writing session, using the notes to write a completed prose piece.

● Depending on the genre, e.g. *report, recount, explanation*, draw the children's attention to the organisational and structural features, e.g. an opening definition, *Armour is special clothing to protect the body*, a closing summary.

● Discuss the reasons for starting new sections marked by a heading, e.g. *Who wore armour?* or new paragraphs marked by a line space or indentation.

Group

● In pairs the children use their own note grids from **Y4 T2 T16, 17** to write a factual prose piece.

● Ask the children to present their findings in an alternative way from prose, e.g. chart, labelled diagrams. Mount both pieces together.

● Ask the children to compare both forms of presentation. Discuss which they think is best and why.

Plenary

● When sharing the finished work, explicitly discuss the ways the children structured their prose, looking at headings, paragraphs, etc.

Relevant published materials/resources

NLS Activity Resource Sheet

Year	4
Term	3
Strand	T 16 – 18

Objectives

To read, compare and evaluate examples of arguments and discussions. How arguments are presented; how statistics, graphs, etc. can be used to support arguments. From examples of persuasive writing, to investigate how style and vocabulary are used to convince the intended reader.

Activities

N.B.
You will need to have collected a series of texts on a particular issue, e.g. building a fifth terminal at Heathrow, the banning fox hunting bill.
Create a display, from which texts can be removed, and encourage children to contribute.

Class

● Select one or two texts from the display. Enlarge these on an OHT and provide multiple copies if possible.
● In Shared Reading discuss how arguments are developed.
● Highlight:
  - the point of the argument;
  - further details and evidence;
  - facts and opinions;
  - use of connectives, e.g. however, because, never-the-less, so;
  - graphs and charts, and the visual presentation of the data;
  - pictures chosen to support the case.

Group

● In pairs the children 'deconstruct' the text studied in the whole-class introduction, using the Photocopiable Resource Sheet.
● They repeat this activity with another text selected from the display, if possible taking the opposite point of view.

Relevant published materials/resources

Issues, Magic Bean In-Fact (Heinemann).**Ian and Fred's Big Green Book** (David Bennett Publishing).

NLS Activity Resource Sheet

Objectives

To evaluate advertisements for their impact, appeal and honesty, focusing in particular on how information about the product is presented. To design an advertisement, such as a poster or radio jingle on paper or screen, making use of linguistic and other features learnt from reading examples.

Activities

N.B.
You will need to have collected a series of advertisements on a theme, e.g. toys, books, sweets, cars. Mount a display and encourage the children to add to it. Keep a note of where the advertisements came from as this provides evidence of the intended audience.
You will need to use the advertisements from the display or have duplicates.

Class

● Enlarge an advertisement on OHT or provide multiple copies.
● Discuss the advertisement, drawing attention to the image, headline, how it attracts attention, persuasive language, actual hard facts compared with rhetoric, etc.
● Annotate the advertisement and discuss it.

Group

● Stick the advertisements on a larger sheet. Ask pairs of children to annotate as in the class activity.
● Provide the children with a picture of an item, e.g. washing-up liquid, to advertise. Ask them to annotate the picture and write a persuasive text for it. Then compare this with the original. Conversely, give the children the text and ask them to add the image.
● Give the children an image, e.g. the latest electronic toy. Ask them to write the text for publication in a child's magazine. Next, suggest that they write an alternative text for a parents' magazine.
● Write an advertisement for your school.
● Go through the text of an advertisement, underlining all the adjectives and adverbs. Replace these with *negative* alternatives. Compare the effects.

Extension

● Look at classified advertisements in newspapers to examine how they are designed.

Relevant published materials/resources

NLS Activity Resource Sheet

Objectives

To assemble and sequence points in order to plan the presentation of a point of view, e.g. on hunting, school rules.

Activities

Class
- Model a writing session using evidence collected in **Y4 T3 T16–18.**
- Use enlarged 'prompts' for planning, e.g. *We believe that …, This class thinks …, Have you ever considered …?*
- Go through each point logically:

point 1 _____	point 2 _____
evidence _____	evidence _____

- Draw attention to the structure and language features such as logical and causal connectivities, etc. Draw on knowledge discussed in **Y4 T3 T16–18** to come to a conclusion.

Group
- Use the modelled planning from the class lesson to write up as a piece of continuous prose. Use a writing frame, as in the Photocopiable Resource Sheet, for some children if needed.

Relevant published materials/resources

NLS Activity Resource Sheet

Year	5
Term	1
Strand	T 21

Objectives

To identify the features of recounted texts such as sports reports, diaries, police reports, including: introduction to orientate reader; chronological sequence; supporting illustrations; degree of formality adopted; use of connectives, e.g. *first ... next ... once.*

Activities

Class

● Share a clearly structured text to suggest what each part tells the children, e.g. *the introduction – who? what? where? when? why? what happened?*
● Elicit the key connecting phrases/words, e.g. *At first/yesterday/ next/then/finally.* Highlight any time-order words.
● The class can create their own recounted text using the same model of connectives.
● Read a news report, e.g. crime, sport. List any similarities to previous text and highlight them. Read another news report and list similarities. Focus on the key features of recounts, e.g. *introduction, orientation, chronological order, past tense, time connectives, settings, events, conclusions.*
● Read extracts from diaries and investigate their features, i.e. how they differ from recounts in their use of an external ordering system, personal references, shortened forms, etc. Children will readily relate to such 'diary' forms as log books, e.g. *Captain's log: Star Date 3025.*

Group

● Genre exchange. The children can read a recipe or a set of instructions, and translate them to recount. Refer to purpose, audience, key feature. Other possible genres to play with include commentary, advertisement, police report. Peer evaluation during a Plenary session will be important.
● Children should be using their own frames to write their own recount, e.g. a trip, an experiment. This should lead to peer evaluation in a Plenary session.
● Colour-code recount features of several recounted news reports. Sequence a chopped-up report. Use features as cues.
● Children could read a present-tense version of a recount, and suggest why it does not work and alter to the past tense. Edit this version to a past-tense recount.
● Translate the diary extracts into a full version and vice versa. Continue to structure, using a recount frame if appropriate for some children.

Relevant published materials/resources

The First Lunar Landing, Magic Bean In-Fact (Heinemann). **Discovery World** (Heinemann).

NLS Activity Resource Sheet

Objectives

To read and evaluate a range of instructional texts in terms of their: purposes; organisation and layout; clarity and usefulness.

Activities

Class
- Through discussion, establish the purpose and audience of text, either using a Big Book, real-life texts, e.g. a selection of recipes, or both.
- Investigate with the children the organisation, e.g. title, ingredients, method, of the text (the content relevant to the purpose) and the layout (how the content is arranged). List the key features under organisation and layout.
- Investigate the kinds of verbs commonly found in instruction texts, e.g. imperatives (commands), often 'action' words.

Group
- Provide a range of procedural texts, e.g. a range of recipes. Children should have a sheet with two headings:

Organisation	Layout

They should look at the text and note features under the appropriate headings.
- Some children can explore the texts to highlight the various ingredient lists. They can then discuss these lists and compare them. Are ingredients always the same kind of thing?
- Some children go through texts underlining verbs. They can sort them out under two headings – commands, other verbs. Discuss their findings during the Plenary session.
- Later all children should try to write their own instructions relating to activities they are carrying out elsewhere in the curriculum. Group revision and evaluation should focus on the extent to which they use appropriate forms, whether they are clear, etc.

Relevant published materials/resources

Writing Frames, David Wray and Maureen Lewis (Reading and Language Information Centre, Reading University). **Keeping Silkworms,** Magic Bean In-Fact (Heinemann). **Discovery World** (Heinemann).

NLS Activity Resource Sheet

Objectives

To read a range of explanatory texts, investigating and noting features of impersonal style, e.g. complex sentences: use of the passive voice; technical vocabulary; hypothetical language *(if ... then, might, when the ...)*; use of phrases to make sequential, causal, logical connections, e.g. while, during, after, because, due to, only when, so.

Activities

Class

● Prepare a large version of a sample text from an information book you are using in your curriculum work (perhaps in science or history). An enlarged, photocopied version might do, or a version on an OHT.
● Discuss with the class how you can tell this is an information text and not a piece of fiction.
● Draw out features, e.g.:

---

1. Impersonal style - i.e. phrases such as 'it is thought ...', 'the Tudors were ...', 'rain is formed ...'. Contrast this with the personal style found in fiction: 'I felt ...', 'we really wanted ...'.

2. Use of passive voice - i.e. 'volcanoes are formed from ...', 'the Spartans were beaten by ...'. Contrast these with active constructions and discuss what difference these make to the text.

3. Use of connectives - talk about types of connectives, e.g. logical (because, on account of, therefore) and contrast with chronological (first, next, after that).

● Mark each of these features with a separate colour highlighter pen.
● List these three features on the board.

Group

● Groups can investigate other texts of various kinds and, using photocopies, mark examples of the above features on these texts.

Plenary

● Discuss the groups' findings, using texts to review the features discussed.

Relevant published materials/resources

NLS Activity Resource Sheet

Year	5
Term	2
Strand	T 20, 21

Objectives

Notemaking: to discuss what is meant by 'in your own words' and when it is appropriate to copy, quote and adapt. To convert personal notes into notes for others to read, paying attention to appropriateness of style, vocabulary and presentation.

Activities

Class

● Using an enlarged text (either photocopied or on OHT), read together with the children and discuss what items of information in this text are essential and which are less crucial.
● Use a highlighter pen to mark the essential items and then extract these as a series of notes on the text.
● Discuss the various features in the text and in note taking which enable this to be done:

> 1. Key words
> 2. Headings and sub-headings
> 3. Substituting short phrases for long sentences
> 4. Summarising

● Ilustrate all of these using the enlarged text.

Group

● Group can try out note taking on a text relevant to their work. They might do this as a game, with the object of seeing who can express the essence of a text in the fewest words.
● Another group can work from some notes to try to reconstruct what the original text might have said.
● Another group can investigate e-mail acronyms and suggest what the following might stand for:
AFAIR (as far as I remember), **BFN** (bye for now), **ISTR** (I seem to remember), **IMHO** (in my humble opinion), **ASAP** (as soon as possible), **ROTFL** (rolling on the floor laughing). There are many others like this that can be used.
● Another group can explore small ads. and draw up a list of shorthand forms, e.g.
amc (all modern conveniences), **hcw** (hot and cold water), **ono** (or nearest offer), **sae** (stamped, addressed envelope), **sem.det**. (semi-detached).

Relevant published materials/resources

NLS Activity Resource Sheet

Year	5
Term	3
Strand	T 12,13

To read and evaluate letters, e.g. from newspapers, magazines, intended to inform, protest, complain, persuade, considering (i) how they are set out, (ii) how language is used ... ;
to read other examples, e.g. newspaper comment, headlines, adverts, fliers, etc. Compare writing which informs and persuades ... .

Activities

Class

● Use an enlarged text taken from a newspaper that is intended to persuade. Letters, editorials, personal columns may be suitable for this.
● Read the text together and discuss with the class which parts of it they feel they should believe and which they feel sceptical about.
● Mark on the text elements that are intended to persuade the reader. You might focus on:

> 1. The text's layout – where is the eye immediately drawn and why?
> 2. The information presented in the text – why was that information selected and other items not?
> 3. The choice of vocabulary in the text – what is the effect of certain words being used?
> 4. The use of opinion – are opinions clearly marked as such or are they disguised to look like fact?

● Repeat the activity above but use two texts, taken from different sources, each of which gives a slightly different view of the facts.
● Discuss with the class the viewpoints from which these texts are written and how you can tell.

Group

● Some children can repeat the activity in their groups, using different texts. Others can try writing their own persuasive texts, using some of the 'tricks' they have been discovering.
● Other groups can explore a range of text presentation devices such as bullet points, numbered lists, sub-headings, dropped capitals. All of these will be found in magazines and newspapers and the children can discuss and speculate on their purpose before trying to incorporate them in their own writing.

Plenary

● You will need to discuss thoroughly the issues that arise as children explore and attempt to write persuasively.

Relevant published materials/resources

NLS Activity Resource Sheet

Year	5
Term	3
Strand	T 19

Objectives

To construct an argument in note form or full text to persuade others of a point of view and present the case to the class or a group; evaluate its effectiveness.

Activities

Class
- Remind class of work previously done on investigating persuasive text.
- Make a list on the chalkboard of the features discussed, such as layout, inclusion or omission of information, choice of vocabulary.
- Ask for a suggestion of something they feel strongly about which they would like to persuade someone else about.
- Get them to brainstorm some of the points they would make in their argument, using a planning frame, as in the Photocopiable Resource Sheet, if required.
- In Shared Writing, work on a big version of an argument frame, using the Photocopiable Resource Sheet to put these points into a coherent and persuasive order.

Group
- Groups can go through this process again with other issues, using frames as necessary.

Plenary
- Children can share their final texts and discuss what makes them more or less effective as persuasive writing.

Relevant published materials/resources

Writing Frames, M. Lewis and D. Wray (Reading and Language Information Centre, Reading University).

NLS Activity Resource Sheet

Year	6
Term	1
Strand	T 11

Objectives

To distinguish between biography and autobiography; recognising the effect on the reader of the choice between first and third person; distinguishing between fact, opinion and fiction; distinguishing between implicit and explicit points of view and how these can differ.

Activities

Class

● In a Shared Reading session, using Big Books or multiple copies of books, draw the children's attention to the similarities between biographies and autobiographies.
● Ask the children to identify the differences, focusing particularly on the point of view of the author.
● Focus on words that identify facts and opinions.

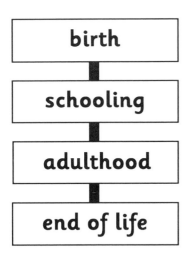

Group

● From photocopied extracts or multiple copies of books, ask the children to find and record examples of facts and opinions. Use the Photocopiable Resource Sheet 'Facts and Opinions' for recording.
● Give the children a copy of the Photocopiable Resource Sheet 'Planning a Biography'. Ask them to research the biographies/autobiographies to track the main events in the life of the subject. They could then plot this information onto a time-line.

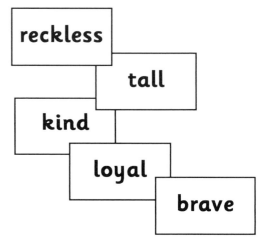

Plenary

● Build up a bank of words to describe the subject's physical appearance and personality.

Relevant published materials/resources

NLS Activity Resource Sheet

Year	6
Term	1
Strand	T 11

Objectives

To distinguish between biography and autobiography: recognising the effect on the reader of the choice between first and third person; distinguishing between fact, opinion and fiction; distinguishing between implicit and explicit points of view and how these can differ.

Activities

Class

- Introduce children to either an autobiography or a biography in a Shared Reading session using a Big Book or multiple copies.
- Ask the children to identify characteristics, e.g. *structure, language features, organisational devices* that are common to recounts.
- Examine diagrams, e.g. family trees, and illustrations/photos of people, events and artefacts.
- Focus on facts and opinions.
- Focus on who is the author. How might this influence what is written?

Group

- Distribute examples of autobiographies or biographies in as many different formats as possible.
- Ask the children to examine their text to check whether it has the identified characteristics and whether further common characteristics are evident.

Plenary

- Produce a wall display of the characteristics found in autobiographies or biographies.
- Encourage the children to refer and add to the display when studying other autobiographies and biographies.

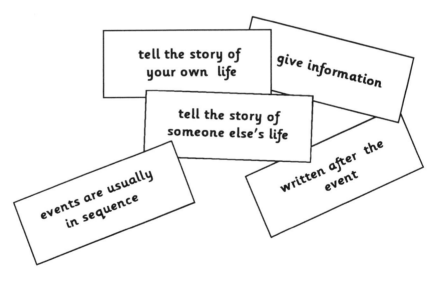

tell the story of your own life

give information

tell the story of someone else's life

written after the event

events are usually in sequence

Relevant published materials/resources

Losing My Roof, Pathways (Collins Ed.). **The Story of Grace Darling,** Pathways (Collins Ed.). **Cousteau** and **Memories** from the Magic Bean In-Fact series (Heinemann).**Tomorrow is a Great Word,** Big Book and standard size format, Magic Bean In-Fact (Heinemann).**The Diary of Anne Frank** and **Zlata's Diary** (Puffin). **Korky Paul, Biography of an Illustrator,** Discovery World (Heinemann).

NLS Activity Resource Sheet

Year	6
Term	1
Strand	T 12

Objectives

To comment critically on the language, style, success of examples of non-fiction such as periodicals, reviews, reports, leaflets.

Activities

Class

- Using a variety of examples of reviews, *book, film, music*, etc., discuss the purpose and audience. Examine the structure, drawing the children's attention to the use of paragraphs and specific vocabulary.
- Discuss the impact of the choice of words, e.g. *a stunning film* or *a pleasant film.*
- In modelled writing sessions demonstrate the planning and writing of a review.

Did you see ...?

No, I missed it. Was it good?

Group

- Use the Photocopiable Resource Sheet to examine reviews from newspapers and magazines. Focus on whether they are biased or unbiased, i.e. do they present both positive and negative elements?
- The children write a review of a TV programme, a book or a film, incorporating the points previously covered.

Plenary

- Children read each other's reviews, commenting on whether they now want to read the book or see the film!

Title	I liked it because ...	I didn't like it because ...

Relevant published materials/resources

Reviews from magazines and newspapers of children's books, children's TV programmes, films they may have seen.

NLS Activity Resource Sheet

Year	6
Term	1
Strand	T 14

Objectives

To develop the skills of biographical and autobiographical writing in role, adopting distinctive voices, e.g. of historical characters, through, e.g.: preparing a CV; composing a biographical account based on research; describing a person from different perspectives, e.g. police; description, school report, newspaper obituary.

Activities

N.B.
Read extracts from examples of biographies and autobiographies to the class prior to this activity.

Class

● Demonstrate how to plan and make notes for a piece of autobiographical or biographical writing.
● Brainstorm a list of questions that could be used to interview someone in the class prior to planning their autobiography.
● Model writing in an autobiographical or biographical style. Focus on using the variety of connectives used in recounts.

Where were you born?

How old are you?

Were you ever brave?

My Life

Group

● Using the questions, the children pair up and interview each other, recording their responses. They add other questions they feel are relevant.
● The children write up their interview in an autobiographical style. Use the writing frame on the Photocopiable Resource Sheet to support children who may need it.
● Each child takes on the role of a historical or fictional character to plan and write autobiographies.
● The children research, plan and write biographies of characters encountered in other areas of the curriculum, using a variety of texts, revising, editing and publishing their work.

Relevant published materials/resources

As **Y6 T1 T8**.

NLS Activity Resource Sheet

Objectives

To read and understand examples of official language and its characteristic features ... ; to use reading to investigate conditionals, e.g. using *if ... then, might, could, would,* etc., and their uses, e.g. in deduction, speculation, supposition.

Activities

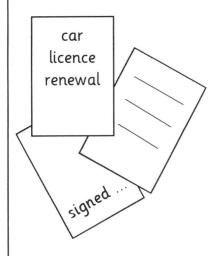

car licence renewal

signed ...

Class

● Collect a variety of official forms, reports, documents, etc. Discuss who would receive these and what response would be required.

● Demonstrate the filling in of a form, a written response to a report, e.g. in the form of a letter or analysis.

● Draw the children's attention to the use of conditional sentences and how specific words change sentence meaning.

● Using a sentence stem, e.g. *if you wish to contact the office you ...* , a variety of conditional words, e.g. *might, could, would,* and a variety of sentence endings, e.g. *press this bell, contact the address below, ask for Mrs. Jones,* explore with the children how sentence meanings change with the use of different conditional words and sentence endings.

Group

● The children write official forms, letters and documents, in the role of a historical or fictitious character, e.g. a letter from Augustus to his soldiers, Mr. Bumble's behaviour rules for breakfast in the workhouse.

● Give the children the Photocopiable Resource Sheet and ask them to explore mixing and matching sentences, using different endings, beginnings and conditional words. How do the sentence meanings change?

● Mount the sentences on a wall display to prompt further discussion.

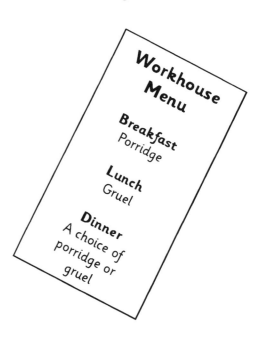

Workhouse Menu

Breakfast
Porridge

Lunch
Gruel

Dinner
A choice of porridge or gruel

Relevant published materials/resources

NLS Activity Resource Sheet

Year	6
Term	2
Strand	T 18,19

Objectives

To construct effective arguments: developing a point logically and effectively; supporting and illustrating points persuasively; anticipating possible objections; harnessing the known views, interests and feelings of the audience; tailoring the writing to formal presentation where appropriate. To write a balanced report of a controversial issue.

Activities

Class

● Demonstrate the planning and drafting of a discussion, e.g. a third runway at Manchester airport, banning football in the playground, using an enlarged copy of the Photocopiable Resource Sheet.

● Use Shared Writing to develop this into a first draft.

● Discuss the structure and language features of the draft, e.g. logical connectives, present tense, clarity of argument, persuasive words.

● Revise the draft in the light of the discussion.

Group

● Give the children a problem or allow them to choose their own. Ask them to plan and draft an argument, using the Photocopiable Resource Sheet, presenting two points of view, for and against.

● Encourage them to read their writing to other groups before revising their drafts.

Plenary

● Plan how to present the finished writing.

Relevant published materials/resources

Issues, Magic Bean In-Fact (Heinemann).

NLS Activity Resource Sheet

Objectives

To secure understanding of the features of explanatory texts from **Y5 T2**.

Activities

Class
- In a Shared Reading session using a Big Book or multiple copies of texts, draw the children's attention to, and discuss the language and grammatical features that contribute to, the impersonal style of writing, e.g. *rarely uses the first person, generic groups rather than individual, technical language, passive sentences.*
- Develop a list of guidelines for writing an explanatory text based on these language and grammatical features.

Group
- Give the children three or four examples of explanatory writing and ask them to analyse those which follow the guidelines and those which do not. Which are the most and least successful?

Plenary
- Ask the children to explain and justify their conclusions.

Relevant published materials/resources

Natural Disasters, Magic Bean In-Fact (Heinemann).

NLS Activity Resource Sheet

Year	6
Term	3
Strand	T 17,18

Objectives

To appraise a text quickly and effectively; to retrieve information from it; to find information quickly and evaluate its value. To secure the skills of skimming, scanning and efficient reading so that research is fast and effective.

Activities

Class

● Using an OHT, model the process of identifying key ideas and words in a text by highlighting or underlining.

● Model note-taking techniques, e.g. recording connected ideas and facts under headings, re-presenting information in diagrammatical, chart or table format, interpreting diagrams, illustrations, etc. in a written format.

● Model the summarising of paragraphs, complex sentences and sequential or ordered points.

● Demonstrate how to work out the meaning of unknown words and terms by referring to surrounding text, same terms in other parts of the text or by using glossaries and dictionaries.

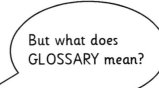

But what does GLOSSARY mean?

Group

● Develop the above skills within the context of research work in other curricular areas.

Find out about me!

how I lived

countries I invaded

how I travelled

Relevant published materials/resources

Note-making posters in the Longman Book Project materials (Longman).

NLS Activity Resource Sheet

Objectives

To secure control of impersonal writing, particularly the sustained use of the present tense and the passive voice. To divide whole texts into paragraphs, paying attention to the sequence of paragraphs and to the links between one paragraph and the next, e.g. through the choice of appropriate connectives.

N.B.
Links with
Y6 T3 T15.

Activities

Class
- In a Shared Reading session reinforce the children's knowledge of the structure and language features of an explanatory text.
- In modelled and Shared Writing sessions demonstrate the planning, drafting and re-drafting of an explanatory text. Focus the children's attention on specific language features, such as use of passive voice, present tense, use of cause and effect connectives, e.g. *because, as, when, this causes, as a result.*

How? Why? Where? ? Who? When?

Group
- Cut copies of explanatory texts into sections and give the children opportunities to reconstruct them using their knowledge of the structure, organisation and cohesion.
- Give the children a subject within their experience, e.g. *Why are rules necessary at school?*
- Ask the group to plan an explanation, using the Photocopiable Resource Sheet if required.
- The children discuss their plans with each other, then draft a full version of their explanations, before collaboratively editing and publishing the final piece.
- Ask the children to write explanations within the context of other curriculum subjects, e.g. science or geography, following the planning, drafting, editing sequence. Encourage the inclusion of diagrams where necessary.

Plenary
- Review the writing, paying specific attention to tense, connectives and voice.

Relevant published materials/resources

How Cows Make Milk, Magic Bean In-Fact series (Heinemann).

Name:

Date:

Writing and drawing

Name:

Date:

Label the face!

Use a ruler to join the labels to the right part of the face.

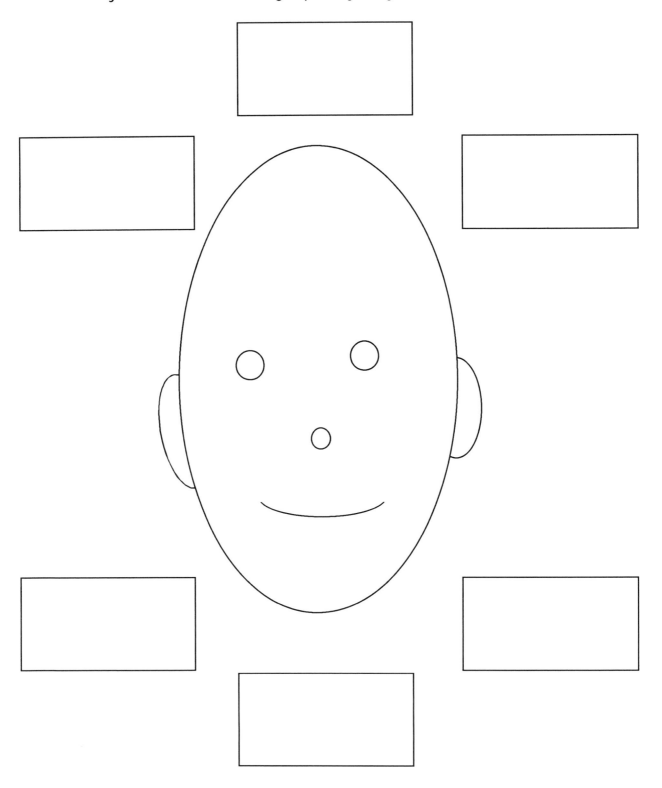

Colour your picture and design a hairstyle for the character.

Photocopiable Resource Sheet **YR T11 B**

Name: _____

Class: _____

On   We

Monday

Tuesday

Wednesday

Thursday

Friday

Name:

Date:

Report writing

Title: _____

What is it?

_____

What does it look like?

_____

Where is it found?

_____

What is it used for?

_____

Ducks	**An exemplar to show a holistic approach to Y1 T3 T17, 19, 22**

Week One **Class** Monday	● Show the children a variety of books about ducks. Ask them to identify what the books are about from the cover and titles. ● Ask the children to brainstorm what they know about ducks and record the answers in column 1 Grid A on the Photocopiable Resource Sheet. Brainstorm what they want to find out about ducks. Record their answers in column 2 of the sheet. ● Select three important questions that you are going to research. Write each question in Grid B, using the Photocopiable Resource Sheet, e.g. *Where do ducks live? What do ducks eat?* ● Read one of the non-fiction books aloud, asking the children to listen out to see if their questions are answered. Record any answers or an X in Grid B. ● Display the grids on the wall in the writing area throughout the two weeks.
Tuesday	● Review the work from the previous day. ● Read a second non-fiction book about ducks, and use Grid B to record any questions answered.
Wednesday	● Review the previous days' work. ● Read a third book about ducks, but this time chose a fiction book. ● Complete Grid B as before and compare answers. ● Discuss which is fact and which is fiction.
Thursday	● Review the previous days' work. ● Re-read each of the three books. ● List any specialist topic words, e.g. *feathers, ducklings*, to create a word bank.
Friday	● Review the previous days' work. ● Re-read each of the three books. ● Focus on the opening sentences. Discuss the differences, e.g. *Once upon a time, This is a duck.*
Week Two **Group** Monday	● Recap the previous week's work using Grid B. ● In Guided Reading sessions, using a group set of **The Life of a Duck** produce a pictorial representation of what has been found out, e.g. picture, diagram. ● Label or write captions (vary according to the ability level). ● Use the class word bank to support the writing.
Tuesday – Thursday	● As above.
Plenary Friday	● Discuss the different ways in which the children have recorded the information. ● Repeat this activity later in the term based on a different theme or collection of books.

Looking at non-fiction books – Grid A

What do we know about …?	What do we want to know about …?

Looking at non-fiction books – Grid B

	Book 1 Title _____	Book 2 Title _____	Book 3 Title _____
Question 1 _____ _____ _____			
Question 2 _____ _____ _____			
Question 3 _____ _____ _____			

Name:

Date:

Following instructions

Choose a variety of instruction texts. Look at the grid. Do your texts show you all these things?

Do the instructions	put things in the right order?	give you a list of what you need?	use language which gives you orders?
Title			
Title			
Title			

Name:

Date:

From one place to another

Where are you starting from?

Where are you going to?

Write or draw directions around the route for your friends to follow.

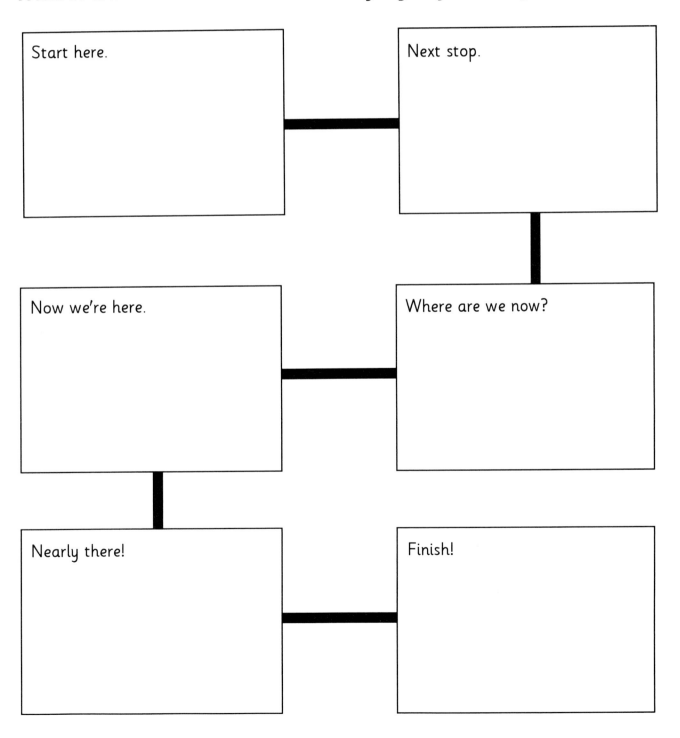

Start here.

Next stop.

Now we're here.

Where are we now?

Nearly there!

Finish!

Name:

Date:

Rules of the game

adult-supported shared writing activity

Name of the game:

Number of players:

Equipment needed:

_____   _____

_____   _____

How do you start the game?

_____

_____

What do you do next?

_____

_____

Write the next three things that you have to do:

1 _____

2 _____

3 _____

Will there be a winner? _____

How will you know when the game is finished?

_____

_____

Definitions

Word	I think it means ...	One dictionary says ...	Another says ...

When you have collected enough words, you can make your own dictionary.

Don't forget to put the words in alphabetical order!

What's in an information book?

Choose a variety of non-fiction books. Look at them carefully then fill in the grid.

Does the book have	a contents page?	an index?	headings?	captions?	diagrams or charts?
Title					
Title					
Title					
Title					

Photocopiable Resource Sheet **Y2 T3 T13**

Name:

Date:

What's going to happen?

Title _____

Author _____

Look at the cover

I think this book will be about:

because:

Check half way through

Is the book

fiction [   ]   non-fiction [   ]

Why would someone read this book?

I think someone would read this book because:

Photocopiable Resource Sheet **Y3 T1 T17 A**

Name:

Date:

Is it fiction or non-fiction?

Choose a book. Look at it carefully.
Tick the box if the book has the features identified.

Title _____

Author _____

blurb ☐

contents page ☐

index ☐

glossary ☐

bibliography ☐

photographs ☐

drawings ☐

diagrams ☐

characters ☐

speech marks ☐

I think this book is:

fiction ☐   non-fiction ☐

because:

Name:

Date:

Comparing fiction and non-fiction

Choose three fiction and three non-fiction books on the same subject. Look at them carefully then fill in the grid.

My subject is _____

What I found out from	fiction or non-fiction?	appearance	habitat	diet	Which of these do I believe?
Title					
Title					
Title					
Title					
Title					
Title					

Name:

Date:

All about my pet

Use the writing frame to write all you know about your pet.

Category	My pet is a …
Name	It is called …
Looks like	It …
Food	It eats …
Life style	On a typical day …
Problems	The main problems with a ——————— are …

Text lucky dip

Your teacher will have given you a collection of texts.
Use the sheet to think about the purpose of your texts and who they were written for.

Text	Purpose (why written)	Audience (who for)

Name:

Date:

Comparing texts

Choose three texts from your class display and use them to fill in the grid.

Type of text	Purpose	Audience	Most important points

Name:

Date:

Is it a fact or an opinion?

Choose and read an article from a newspaper.

Select four statements. Decide whether each statement is a fact or an opinion. Give reasons for your answers.

Facts	Opinion	Not yet proved – evidence unclear

Comparing events

Look at the reports of the same events from two different newspapers.
Underline the key facts and fill in the chart. Do the facts agree?

	Newspaper 1	Newspaper 2
Event		
Time		
Date		
Place		
Who was involved?		

Name:

Date:

Finding out

List three books from the books in the classroom which you think might help answer your question.

Book   **Author**

Now use a book assessment chart to help you decide which two books will be the most useful.

Name:

Date:

My question is: _____

Book (title, author, publisher)	What clues to the content does the cover contain?	Contents page Yes or no?	Key word mentioned?	Index Y/N?	Key word?	Headings Y/N?	Key word?	Illustrations Any of our subject? Give page number.	Our rating Not useful. Useful. Very useful.

Name:
Date:

Note taking grid – A

Question	Answer	Details	Source

Note taking grid – B

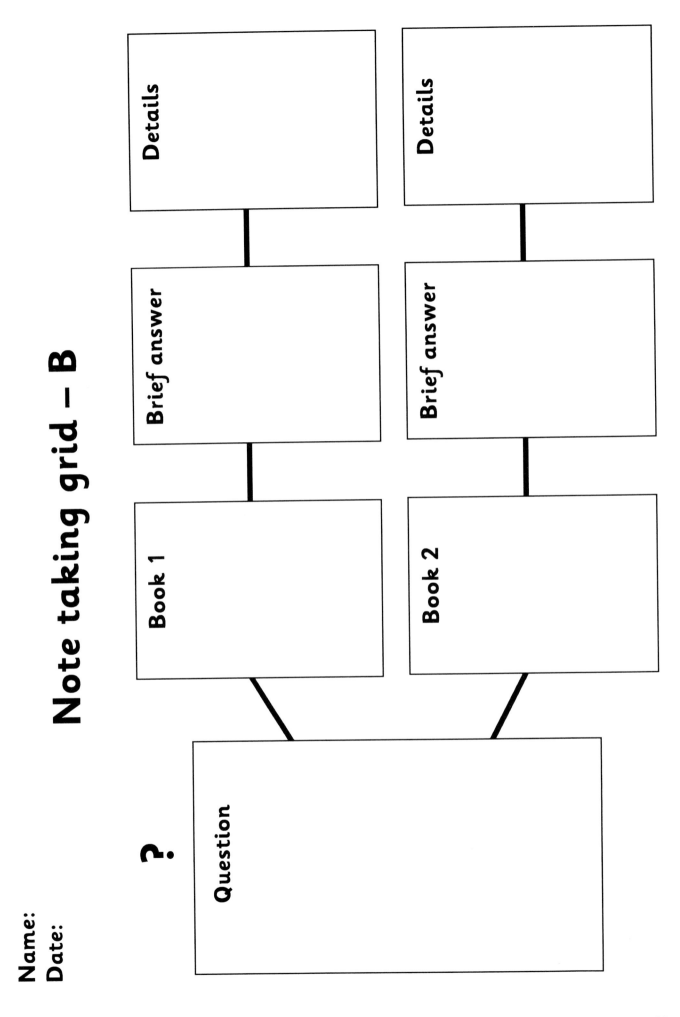

| Book 1 | Brief answer | Details |

| Book 2 | Brief answer | Details |

?

Question

Name:

Date:

Note taking grid – C

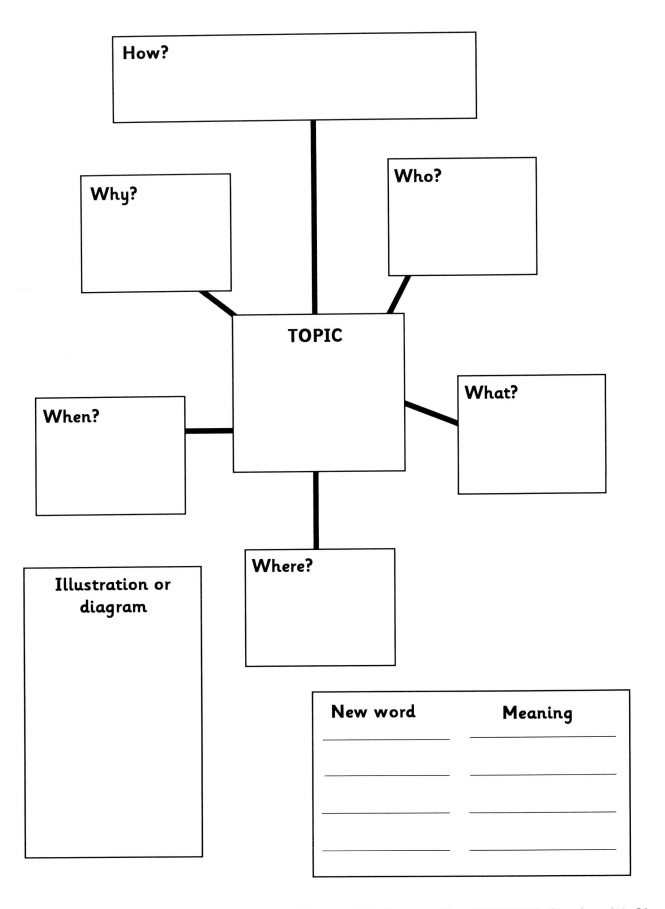

How?

Why?

Who?

TOPIC

When?

What?

Where?

Illustration or
diagram

New word	Meaning

Photocopiable Resource Sheet **Y4 T2 T15–17**

Name:
Date:

Arguments

Argument	Evidence	Our comments
Pictures used		

Name:

Date:

Points of view

There is a lot of debate about ...

Some people, such as ...
say that ...

They also claim ...

However, other groups, such as ....
disagree. They say ...

They argue that ...

After looking at both sides of the debate, I think ...

Photocopiable Resource Sheet **Y4 T3 T21** 83

Name:

Date:

Planning my reasons

I believe that _____

Here are some reasons for this:

Name:

Date:

Argument frame

Some people might argue that

_____

but I think that _____

_____

for several reasons.

One reason is that _____

_____

_____

A further reason is that _____

_____

_____

Furthermore _____

_____

_____

Therefore, although some people think _____

_____

I think I have shown _____

_____

Fact or opinion?

Subject:

Source:

Author:

Find four statements about your chosen subject or character. Decide if you think the statements are fact or opinion. Explain why you think this.

Statement:

Fact? ☐   Opinion? ☐

because:

_____

_____

_____

Statement:

Fact? ☐   Opinion? ☐

because:

_____

_____

_____

Statement:

Fact? ☐   Opinion? ☐

because:

_____

_____

_____

Statement:

Fact? ☐   Opinion? ☐

because:

_____

_____

_____

Name:

Date:

Planning a biography –
the main events in the life of:

_____

Early life – date and place of birth, parents, schooling, friends, etc.

An event – date and place, who was involved, why it was important, etc.

Another event – date and place, who was involved, why it was important, etc.

Another event – date and place, who was involved, why it was important, etc.

Old age – place, infirmity, carers, date of death, etc.

Name:

Date:

The main events

Find out the main events in the life of your chosen subject, using a range of biographies and autobiographies. Find out the dates and record the events in the order that they happened.

My chosen subject is: _____

Date:		Event:

Compare your findings with the other children in your group. Did they find out anything different? Plot your findings on a time-line for the classroom wall.

Name:

Date:

Looking at reviews

A review of:

Source:

Reviewer:

Chose four statements made by the reviewer about the subject. Do the statements give a good or bad opinion? Explain why you think this.

Statement:

Positive? [ ]   Negative? [ ]

because:

_____

_____

Statement:

Positive? [ ]   Negative? [ ]

because:

_____

_____

Statement:

Positive? [ ]   Negative? [ ]

because:

_____

_____

Statement:

Positive? [ ]   Negative? [ ]

because:

_____

_____

Does the reviewer give a biased or unbiased view of the subject?
Discuss what you think with the rest of your group.

Conditional words

Cut up the boxes. Mix and match the sentences. Does the meaning of the sentence change if you use a different conditional word?

Beginnings:

If you wish to contact the office, you ...

When you have filled in the form, you ...

Once you have finished reading your book, you ...

When you reach the zebra crossing, you ...

Conditional words:

might

must

could

should

Endings:

... send it to the above address.

... phone during office hours.

... wait for the traffic to stop.

... want to read another one by the same author.

Put your sentences on a classroom wall display. Explain the reasons for your choices.

Name:

Date:

For or against?

The debate is ...

arguments for ...   arguments against ...

Point 1

Evidence

Point 1

Evidence

Point 2

Evidence

Point 2

Evidence

Point 3

Evidence

Point 3

Evidence

So I think that ...

because ...

Name:

Date:

Explanations

Write your subject in the box. Think of six things that would explain your subject to somebody who knew nothing about it. Write them in the speech bubbles.

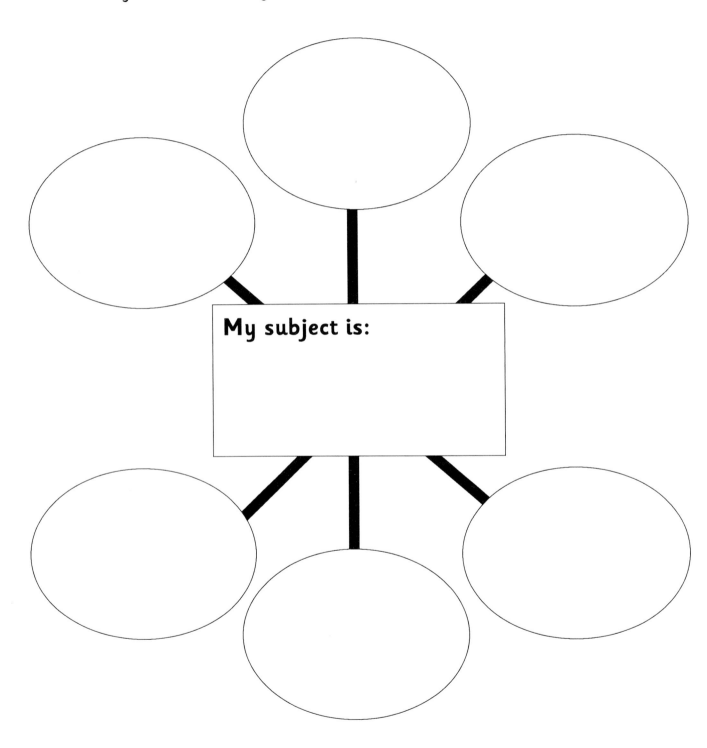

My subject is:

Write a full explanation of your subject, including the ideas in the circles.
Discuss your first draft with a partner.
Think about how you are going to present your work.

Photocopiable Resource Sheet **Y6 T3 T20**